TOPIC

Jesus Is the Healer of My Body and My Soul

SCRIPTURES

1. **John 5:1-9** — After this there was a feast of the Jews, and Jesus went up to Jerusalem. Now there is in Jerusalem by the Sheep Gate a pool, which is called in Hebrew, Bethesda, having five porches. In these lay a great multitude of sick people, blind, lame, paralyzed, waiting for the moving of the water. For an angel went down at a certain time into the pool and stirred up the water; then whoever stepped in first, after the stirring of the water, was made well of whatever disease he had. Now a certain man was there who had an infirmity thirty-eight years. When Jesus saw him lying there, and knew that he already had been in that condition a long time, He said to him, "Do you want to be made well?" The sick man answered Him, "Sir, I have no man to put me into the pool when the water is stirred up; but while I am coming, another steps down before me." Jesus said to him, "Rise, take up your bed and walk." And immediately the man was made well, took up his bed, and walked. And that day was the Sabbath.

2. **Genesis 16:7-10** — Now the Angel of the Lord found her by a spring of water in the wilderness, by the spring on the way to Shur. And He said, "Hagar, Sarai's maid, where have you come from, and where are you going?" She said, "I am fleeing from the presence of my mistress Sarai." The Angel of the Lord said to her, "Return to your mistress, and submit yourself under her hand." Then the Angel of the Lord said to her, "I will multiply your descendants exceedingly, so that they shall not be counted for multitude."

3. **Genesis 16:13** — Then she called the name of the Lord who spoke to her, You-Are-the-God-Who-Sees; for she said, "Have I also here seen Him who sees me?"

4. **John 5:12-15** — Then they asked him, "Who is the Man who said to you, 'Take up your bed and walk'?" But the one who was healed did not know who it was, for Jesus had withdrawn, a multitude being in

that place. Afterward Jesus found him in the temple, and said to him, "See, you have been made well. Sin no more, lest a worse thing come upon you." The man departed and told the Jews that it was Jesus who had made him well.

SYNOPSIS

The four lessons in this study, *Miracles Are for Today*, will focus on the following topics:

- Jesus Is the Healer of My Body and My Soul
- Someone Is Trying To Talk You Out of Your Miracles
- What's on the Other Side of Your 'Yes' to God?
- The Unseen Is Waiting To Be Seen

The Bible is filled with stories about people whose lives were transformed by a miraculous touch from the Lord. One of these people was a man who had made his "home" by the Pool of Bethesda — a haven for the lame and sick who believed the waters of the pool had healing properties. But when Jesus *saw* the man on his sickbed near the pool, it was then that his life was changed. Jesus *saw* this man in his broken state — and Jesus sees you too.

The emphasis of this lesson:

No matter what impossible situation is confronting your life or how long you have been afflicted, Jesus sees you and is ready to set you free! Not only does He want to set you free from the circumstances afflicting you in your natural life, but He wants you to find true freedom in your soul!

Jesus *Saw*

We serve a God who is ALIVE! No other religion can make this claim. Jesus Christ came to earth as God in the flesh, and He is the same today as He was when He first walked on the earth (*see* Hebrews 13:8). Just as Jesus was performing miracles 2,000 years ago, He is still doing the miraculous today! God's miracle-working power has never diminished, and it will *never* diminish.

On the program, Denise shared about a young woman who was diagnosed with a cancerous tumor inside her womb, but she was trusting God and

A Note From Denise Renner

The Word of God is so powerful in our lives. It is essential that every person spend time with God and study His Word in order to stay spiritually strong in these last days.

This study guide corresponds to my *TIME With Denise Renner* TV program by the same title that can be viewed at **deniserenner.org**. My desire is that through these lessons, you find the encouragement and freedom in Christ that you need. I believe the Holy Spirit is going to speak to you through the words you read in this study tool and that as you begin to use it, you will be *propelled* into the abundant life God has planned for you. I encourage you to make the effort to receive all He has for you and all He wants to do in you — it will definitely be worth it!

Whether you have walked with the Lord a long time or have just begun to follow Him, there is so much He wants to give you from His Word. He sees where you are, and He wants to meet you there.

> Therefore do not worry about tomorrow, for tomorrow
> will worry about its own things.
> Sufficient for the day is its own trouble.
> — Matthew 6:34

Your sister and friend in Jesus Christ,

Denise Renner

Denise Renner

Miracles Are for Today

Published by Rick Renner Ministries
www.renner.org

ISBN 13: 978-1-6675-0602-9

eBook ISBN 13: 978-1-6675-0603-6

His Word for her healing. When she went for a follow-up appointment, the doctor who was examining her said, "We can't see anything! There's nothing there! It's like it just disappeared!" The power of God entered her womb and that tumor simply vanished! That is a miracle!

Denise also shared about the miracle God performed in her own life.

> I had a disease for 13 years that affected the skin on my face. I was embarrassed about the way I looked, and I felt ashamed and inferior to everyone else. But when I heard "By His stripes we were healed," something inside clicked, faith arose in my heart, and I believed healing would come. Several months passed, and one night I went to bed as always. I don't know how He did it, but I woke up the next morning and my forehead, cheeks, and neck were completely healed. After 13 long years, my skin was clear. The disease was gone! That is the miracle-working power of God!

In the Bible, we read about a man who had been suffering from an infirmity for 38 years. His testimony begins in John 5:1-6:

"After this there was a feast of the Jews, and Jesus went up to Jerusalem. Now there is in Jerusalem by the Sheep Gate a pool, which is called in Hebrew, Bethesda, having five porches. In these lay a great multitude of sick people, blind, lame, paralyzed, waiting for the moving of the water. For an angel went down at a certain time into the pool and stirred up the water; then whoever stepped in first, after the stirring of the water, was made well of whatever disease he had.

"Now a certain man was there who had an infirmity thirty-eight years. When Jesus saw him lying there, and knew that he already had been in that condition a long time, He said to him, 'Do you want to be made well?'"

In the time before Jesus went to the Cross to pay the price for sin, sickness, and disease, very few people received healing. There was a pool in Bethesda where an angel would occasionally descend and stir up the water. Whenever this happened, whoever first stepped into the pool as the waters moved would be healed.

There was a great multitude of sick, blind, lame, and paralyzed people surrounding the pool, but Jesus *saw* this particular man. Every one of those individuals lying by the pool was hoping to be the first in the pool to receive healing, but again, Jesus saw this particular man who had suffered for 38 long years with this infirmity.

The God Who Sees

God's eyes were also on an Egyptian handmaiden named Hagar. In the Old Testament, we read of Abraham — the "father of faith" — and his wife Sarah. Unable to conceive a child, Sarah gave her handmaiden, Hagar, to Abraham to bear a child. However, when Hagar became pregnant, Sarah began treating her with contempt because she had yet to conceive a child of her own. In response to Sarah's harsh treatment, Hagar fled to the wilderness.

Genesis 16:7-10 says, "Now the Angel of the Lord found her by a spring of water in the wilderness, by the spring on the way to Shur. And He said, 'Hagar, Sarai's maid, where have you come from, and where are you going?' She said, 'I am fleeing from the presence of my mistress Sarai.' The Angel of the Lord said to her, 'Return to your mistress, and submit yourself under her hand.' Then the Angel of the Lord said to her, 'I will multiply your descendants exceedingly, so that they shall not be counted for multitude.'"

The Angel of the Lord then revealed to Hagar that she would bear a son and that she was to name him Ishmael, "Because the Lord has heard your affliction" (Genesis 16:11). Verse 13 continues, "Then she called the name of the Lord who spoke to her, You-Are-the-God-Who-Sees; for she said, 'Have I also here seen Him who sees me?'"

Our God is the God Who Sees! Just as God saw Hagar in the wilderness, and Jesus saw the man at the Pool of Bethesda, Jesus sees you and me today. If you are battling sickness or disease — He sees. If you are struggling financially — He sees. If you have a broken heart — He sees. What's incredible about God, our Heavenly Father, is His ability to *see* and *understand* any adversity confronting us.

Rise, Take Up Your Bed, and Walk

Let's return to the story about the man by the Pool of Bethesda. Jesus saw this man and asked him a simple question: "Do you want to be made well?" (v. 6) But the man did not answer with a simple *yes*, he could only answer with what he knew and had seen with his own eyes. John 5:7-9 continues, "The sick man answered Him, 'Sir, I have no man to put me into the pool when the water is stirred up; but while I am coming, another steps down before me.' Jesus said to Him, 'Rise, take up your bed and walk.' And immediately the man was made well, took up his bed, and walked. And that day was the Sabbath."

When the man explained to Jesus that He had no one to put him into the water when it stirred, he was basically describing his impossible situation. This man did not know who Jesus was and didn't recognize that He was the Messiah. His faith was not in Jesus; his faith was in an angel stirring the water and the hope that someone would help him be the first to get into the water when the water was stirred. But Jesus had something else in mind. He said, "Rise, take up your bed and walk," and the man was immediately made well.

Everything this man had ever known was his debilitating physical condition, his hopelessness, his "no way out," and his inability to get into that water. But as Jesus spoke, the power of God manifested through His words: "Rise, take up your bed and walk!" What a powerful moment! The man had been crippled for 38 years of his life, and in one moment, as the power of God manifested through Jesus' words, this man was immediately healed!

If you are a believer in Jesus Christ, the Holy Spirit is in you; He is the miracle-working power of God who resides inside you! When we choose to put our focus and our faith upon the truth that "by His stripes we are healed" (Isaiah 53:5), the power of God will manifest in our physical body regardless of what we are facing. We may not even be aware that it has happened, but suddenly we are free from that sickness and disease! Somewhere between the problem and the miracle is the love, mercy, grace, and miracle-working power of God!

A Religious Response to a Miracle

There was a barrier between the man by the Pool of Bethesda and his healing; that barrier was his complete inability to help himself. When Jesus *saw* him in the midst of the great multitude surrounding him, the man had no idea who Jesus was, nor did he believe in Him. But that did not change the fact that power was ready to be released through Jesus.

Although this man was miraculously healed, he had no idea who it was that had healed him. And instead of rejoicing over the man's freedom from his disease, the Pharisees were angry and critical. John 5:10-13 describes the events that followed this man's healing.

"The Jews therefore said to him who was cured, 'It is the Sabbath; it is not lawful for you to carry your bed.' He answered them, 'He who made me well said to me, "Take up your bed and walk."'" Then they asked him, 'Who is the Man who said to you, "Take up your bed and walk"?' But the one who was healed did not know who it was, for Jesus had withdrawn, a multitude being in that place."

Imagine if *you* were stuck by this pool for 38 years waiting for an angel to stir the waters and hoping you would be the first in the pool to be healed. Imagine one day while watching for the waters to stir, a man whom you had never seen or heard of before, tells you to pick up your bed and walk. To your astonishment, you are instantly healed, and you pick up your bed to walk home! But instead of the religious leaders being excited about your miracle, they are more concerned that a man healed you on the Sabbath and that you're walking around with your bed on a holy day. They missed the miracle!

Healed *and* Redeemed

When Jesus went to the Cross, He took our sicknesses and He took our diseases, but He also took all of our sin upon Himself so we would not spend eternity in eternal punishment and separated from God. In fact, He *became* sin and took our punishment upon Himself! Yes, Jesus desires to heal you, but He also wants to touch your heart — to redeem you.

What an amazing, exciting, and miraculous healing the man at the pool of Bethesda received from Jesus! He had been set free from the physical restrictions in his body that had kept him bound for 38 years. But Jesus not only cared about this man's physical condition, but He was also concerned about his spiritual condition; He cared about what was on the inside of that man. Jesus could have simply healed the man and never interacted with him again, but Jesus cared so much that He went searching for Him.

John 5:14 and 15 says, "Afterward Jesus found him in the temple, and said to him, 'See, you have been made well. Sin no more, lest a worse thing come upon you.' The man departed and told the Jews that it was Jesus who had made him well."

The Bible says that we did not choose Jesus, but He chose us (*see* John 15:16). Jesus was looking for me when I gave Him my whole life, my heart, and my soul! Jesus was looking for me, and He was looking for you! We did not come to Him on our own; He searched for us, and He came to us!

Complete Redemption

The man at the Bethesda pool was not looking for Jesus, but Jesus was looking for him, and He found him! After healing the man, Jesus told him, "Sin no more..." (John 5:14). Jesus was speaking out of His mercy and told him to stop sinning because He did not want that man to suffer something worse than he had already experienced. Jesus did not reveal the man's sin to others, but I believe the man knew exactly what Jesus meant.

You and I need to heed the warnings of the Holy Spirit on the inside when He speaks to our heart. He may ask us to change a bad attitude, forgive someone who has wronged us, or give up something that is not beneficial to our walk with Him. Jesus may have healed your body, but He wants you to continue to be transformed on the inside through His Word and by His Spirit.

When Jesus died on the Cross, He died for the *whole* man; He died not only for our physical healing but for our redemption. His desire is for us to have soundness of mind, to bear the fruit of His Spirit, and to become loving and forgiving toward others. And the same power that healed that man who had been bound for 38 years is the same power that is available to redeem and heal you today. He is still speaking today. He is there for you, and all you need to do is reach out and receive!

STUDY QUESTIONS

Be diligent to present yourself approved to God, a worker who does not need to be ashamed, rightly dividing the word of truth.
— 2 Timothy 2:15

1. What do you think Jesus saw in the man who had suffered 38 years with his infirmity and why do you think He saw *that* man specifically? Explain your answer.
2. What does the story of Hagar in the wilderness reveal about the character of God? Use one verse from the New Testament to support your answer.

PRACTICAL APPLICATION

But be doers of the word,
and not hearers only, deceiving yourselves.
—James 1:22

Cultivate commitment as you run your race.

1. Are you facing an impossibility in your life? What truth from God's Word are you putting into practice to see your miracle manifest?

2. Take a moment to examine your heart. Are there any areas where old beliefs have entered into your thoughts? If yes, describe that area and how you will change wrong thinking.

LESSON 2

TOPIC

Someone Is Trying To Talk You Out of Your Miracles

SCRIPTURES

1. **John 9:1-15** — Now as Jesus passed by, He saw a man who was blind from birth. And His disciples asked Him saying, "Rabbi, who sinned, this man or his parents, that he was born blind?" Jesus answered, "Neither this man nor his parents sinned, but that the works of God should be revealed in him. I must work the works of Him who sent Me while it is day; the night is coming when no one can work. As long as I am in the world, I am the light of the world." When He had said these things, He spat on the ground and made clay with the saliva; and He anointed the eyes of the blind man with the clay And He said to him, "Go, wash in the pool of Siloam" (which is translated, Sent). So he went and washed, and came back seeing. Therefore the neighbors and those who previously had seen that he was blind said, "Is not this not he who sat and begged?" Some said, "This is he." Others said, "He is like him." He said, "I am he." Therefore they said to him, "How were your eyes opened?" He answered and said, "A Man called Jesus made clay and anointed my eyes and said to me, 'Go to the pool of Siloam and wash.'

So I went and washed, and I received sight." Then they said to him, "Where is He?" He said, "I do not know." They brought him who was formerly blind to the Pharisees. Now it was a Sabbath when Jesus made clay and opened his eyes. Then the Pharisees also asked him again how he had received his sight. He said to them, "He put clay on my eyes, and I washed, and I see."

2. **John 9:20-41** — His parents answered them and said, "We know that this is our son, and that he was born blind, but by what means he now sees we do not know, or who opened his eyes we do not know. He is of age; ask him. He will speak for himself." His parents said these things because they feared the Jews, for the Jews had agreed already that if anyone confessed that He was Christ, he would be put out of the synagogue. Therefore his parents said, "He is of age; ask him." So they again called the man who was blind, and said to him, "Give God the glory! We know that this Man is a sinner." He answered and said, "Whether He is a sinner or not I do not know. One thing I know: that though I was blind, now I see." Then they said to him again, "What did He do to you? How did He open your eyes?" He answered them, "I told you already, and you did not listen. Why do you want to hear it again? Do you also want to become His disciples?" Then they reviled him and said, "You are His disciple, but we are Moses' disciples. We know that God spoke to Moses; as for this fellow, we do not know where He is from." The man answered and said to them, "Why, this is a marvelous thing, that you do not know where He is from; yet He has opened my eyes! Now we know that God does not hear sinners; but if anyone is a worshiper of God and does His will, He hears him. Since the world began it has been unheard of that anyone opened the eyes of one who was born blind. If this Man were not from God, He could do nothing." They answered and said to him, "You were completely born in sins, and are you teaching us?" And they cast him out. Jesus heard that they had cast him out; and when He had found him, He said to him, "Do you believe in the Son of God?" He answered and said, "Who is He, Lord, that I may believe in Him?" And Jesus said to him, "You have both seen Him and it is He who is talking with you." Then he said, "Lord, I believe!" And he worshiped Him. And Jesus said, "For judgment I have come into this world, that those who do not see may see, and that those who see may be made blind." Then some of the Pharisees who were with Him heard these words, and said to Him, "Are we blind also?" Jesus said to them, "If

you were blind, you would have no sin; but now you say, 'We see."
Therefore your sin remains.

SYNOPSIS

Jesus healed a man who was blind from birth; it was a miraculous healing from blindness that had never occurred in the history of Israel. But Jesus not only cared about the blind man regaining his physical sight, He also purposed to seek him out over concern for the man's *spiritual* blindness. Jesus found him, and the man's spiritual eyes were opened to acknowledge that Jesus was his Lord and Savior.

The emphasis of this lesson:

Jesus provided physical healing for all who will believe and receive. More importantly, Jesus made a way for our spiritual eyes to be opened to see. We must not be moved by negative circumstances or the reactions of those surrounding us, and we must not allow anything or anyone to talk us out of our miracle from God! We must guard against religion clouding our eyes to the truth that sets us free!

Who Sinned?

In John 9, we are introduced to a man who was born blind. The miraculous story unfolds in this encouraging chapter as Jesus opens the man's blind eyes, but his healing captured the attention of the disciples and the Pharisees. John 9:1 begins, "Now as Jesus passed by, He saw a man who was blind from birth."

Many of us are blessed with the ability to see and can only imagine what it would be like to be blind. But this particular man was born blind and had only known darkness his entire life. He had never seen the blue of a clear sky or the grey of a stormy sea. He had never seen the shades of green in the wide variety of trees in this world nor the vast colors of the many types of flowers. He had never seen the pure white of newly fallen snow nor the evening glow of the moon and stars in the heavens above our world. He had never seen the faces of his mother or father or wife or child. He could hear their voices and touch them with his hands and even embrace them, but his world was void of light.

While passing this blind man, the disciples began to question Jesus, assuming that sin was the reason the man was blind. They asked,

"…Rabbi, who sinned, this man or his parents, that he was born blind?" (John 9:2) The disciples were sincere in their question but wrong in their assumptions. Jesus responded to the disciples' question: "…Neither this man nor his parents sinned, but that the works of God should be revealed in him. I must work the works of Him who sent Me while it is day; the night is coming when no one can work. As long as I am in the world, I am the light of the world" (John 9:4-6). Jesus then *demonstrated* — to His disciples, the blind man, and all who were listening — the powerful works of God.

Jesus declared Himself to be the light of the world knowing He was about to bring light to that man's darkness! John 9:6 and 7 continue, "When He had said these things, He spat on the ground and made clay with saliva; and He anointed the eyes of the blind man with the clay. And He said to him, "Go, wash in the pool of Siloam" (which is translated, Sent). So he went and washed, and came back seeing."

The blind man had only heard Jesus' voice, but he was quick to do what he had been instructed to do. He knew that a man named Jesus had put clay on his blind eyes and instructed him to go to the Pool of Siloam to wash the clay away. This man — blind from birth — returned seeing perfectly!

An Uproar in the Neighborhood

You can imagine the commotion this caused among those who knew the "blind beggar." The people had witnessed a miracle! "Therefore the neighbors and those who previously had seen that he was blind said 'Is not this he who sat and begged?' Some said, 'This is he.' Others said, 'He is like him.' He said, "I am he" (John 9:8,9).

The neighbors were shocked. They had known this man all his life. He had been blind and a beggar all the years they had known him, but now he could see everything — including them! He must have been so excited to be able to see the faces of those he spoke to. Until that day, he'd only known the sound of the voices of his neighbors, and now, for the first time, he could look into their eyes. Some people doubted that it was really the same man as the blind man they had always known; they thought maybe it was someone who simply looked like him. But this man cleared up any confusion as to who he was. He clearly stated, "I am he" (v. 9).

But that didn't stop the interrogation of this man whose sight had been restored. John 9:10-12 continues: "Therefore they said to him, 'How were your eyes opened?' He answered and said, 'A Man called Jesus made clay and anointed my eyes and said to me, "Go to the pool of Siloam and wash." So I went and washed, and I received sight. Then they said to him, 'Where is He?' He said, 'I do not know.'"

After instructing the blind man to wash in the pool of Siloam, Jesus quietly departed. Just like He did after He told the crippled man at the pool of Bethesda to "rise and walk," Jesus slipped away, trying not to gather a crowd. But the people were shocked that the man they had known to be blind was now seeing. They wanted to know how it had happened and who it was that had given him sight, so the people decided to take this once-blind man to the Pharisees.

John 9:13 and 14 recounts, "They brought him who formerly was blind to the Pharisees. Now it was the Sabbath when Jesus made the clay and opened his eyes." Again, we see the Pharisees' attention was directed to the Law instead of the miracle that was before them.

Questions, Questions, and More Questions

The Pharisees were a sect of Jews who taught that to reach God required strict adherence to Jewish Law. They were teachers and enforcers of the Law, but Jesus called them hypocrites (*see* Matthew 23:13,27,28). It was in front of this group of Jewish citizens that the once-blind man stood. "Then the Pharisees also asked him again how he had received his sight. He said to them, 'He put clay on my eyes, and I washed, and I see'" (John 9:15).

First, the man's neighbors questioned how his blind eyes were opened, and then the Pharisees peppered him with questions. In the Greek language, the words imply that the Pharisees were interrogating the man. Over and over and over again, they kept asking the man to explain how his sight was restored, who it was who healed him, and to verify who he was.

Finally, the Pharisees believed the man was who he said he was, but they did not believe he was born blind. Needing more information, they decided they would question his parents.

"And they asked them, saying, 'Is this your son, who you say was born blind? How does he now see?' His parents answered them and said, 'We know that this is our son, and that he was born blind; but by what means he now sees we do not know, or who opened his eyes we do not know. He is of age; ask him. He will speak for himself.' His parents said these things because they feared the Jews, for the Jews had agreed already that if anyone confessed that He was Christ, he would be put out of the synagogue. Therefore his parents said, 'He is of age; ask him'" (John 9:19-23).

The parents of the man who had been born blind did not want to be put out of the synagogue by the Pharisees. They were afraid of the consequences of admitting that the man who healed their son might be the Messiah, so they told the Jewish leaders to ask their son since he was old enough to answer for himself. But tensions were starting to rise. The story of this miracle continues in verse 24:

"So they again called the man who was blind, and said to him, 'Give God the glory! We know that this Man is a sinner.' He answered and said, 'Whether He is a sinner or not I do not know. One thing I know: that though I was blind, now I see.'"

"Then they said to him again, 'What did He do to you? How did He open your eyes?' He answered them, 'I told you already, and you did not listen. Why do you want to hear it again? Do you also want to become His disciples?' Then they reviled him and said, 'You are His disciple, but we are Moses' disciples. We know that God spoke to Moses; as for this fellow, we do not know where He is from.'"

"The man answered and said to them, 'Why, this is a marvelous thing, that you do not know where He is from; yet He has opened my eyes! Now we know that God does not hear sinners; but if anyone is a worshiper of God and does His will, He hears him. Since the world began it has been unheard of that anyone opened the eyes of one who was born blind. If this Man were not from God, He could do nothing.'"

"They answered and said to him, 'You were completely born in sins, and are you teaching us?' And they cast him out" (John 9:24-34).

Rejected and Cast Out

This man, who could now see, was innocent. He had no deception in his heart or false motives to speak of. He only knew that a Man he had never met put clay on his eyes and told him to go wash away the clay in the Pool of Siloam. After doing what the Man told him to do, he could see for the first time in his life. And now, instead of rejoicing with him about this miracle, people were interrogating him.

The Pharisees were upset that Jesus healed the man on the Sabbath, which was against Jewish Law, and they wanted to know who He was. The man once again stated his case to the Pharisees, and in essence said, "I don't know who this guy is, but I once was blind and now I see! How can He be a sinner and yet heal my blindness? If He is not from God, He would be unable to give me sight. Since the beginning of time, no one has ever been healed of blindness!" This angered the Pharisees so much that they kicked the man out of the temple.

Friend, know that when you receive your miracle, not everyone will be singing praises with you. People may argue with you about your faith. They may reason that the healing you received was not a miracle from God but that the symptoms simply disappeared on their own. But if you received a miracle from God, no one could argue with you about your personal experience — it is *your* experience.

Not one person could argue with this man who had been born blind but was now able to see! His sight was completely restored. He went from a life of darkness to a world filled with light! The Pharisees were accusing the Man who had healed him of being a sinner because He healed the blind man on the Sabbath. The healed man was astounded that the Pharisees were more concerned about finding the Man who had healed him than they were about the fact that he had been born blind but could now see — something that had never happened!

Do You Believe in the Son of God?

The news that this man had been expelled from the temple reached Jesus, and Jesus went looking for him. This shows the heart and compassion of Jesus. John 9:35-38 says, "Jesus heard that they had cast him out; and when He had found him, He said to him, 'Do you believe in the Son of God?' He answered and said, 'Who is He, Lord, that I may believe in Him?' And Jesus said to him, 'You have both seen Him and it is He who is talking with you.' Then he said, 'Lord, I believe!' And he worshiped Him."

Jesus hates blindness. He went to the Cross and not only took our blindness, but He also took our sicknesses, our diseases, and our pains in His own body. He hates sin and sickness; He punished and defeated it in hell and rose up victoriously! What's so beautiful is that even though Jesus had miraculously healed this man's physical blindness, He later searched for him because He wanted this man to spend eternity with Him in Heaven. Jesus came so man's spiritual eyes would be opened.

Jesus took our sicknesses and diseases on His own body because He did not want us to suffer under them. His compassion was not only to heal our physical bodies but to heal our hearts so we would be born again. The Holy Spirit is revealing Jesus Christ to you. He is the One who gave His life for you, took your sin upon Himself, and made a way for you to spend eternity with Him in Heaven! If you have never received Jesus Christ as your Lord and Savior, I want to provide you the opportunity to make Him the Lord of your life. Just pray this simple prayer from your heart:

> *Father, I ask you to forgive me of my sins. I believe that Jesus is Christ, the Son of God, and that God raised Him from the dead. I turn from my sins and confess Him as my Lord and receive Him as my Savior right now. Amen.*

*If you just prayed that prayer, please let us know. Just call our office at 1-844-473-6637 or send us an email at prayer@deniserenner.org. We want to celebrate with you and welcome you to your new spiritual family!

Blind Eyes

Jesus replied to this man's devotion, and His profound statement is recorded in John 9:39. He said, "…For judgment I have come into this world, that those who do not see may see, and that those who see may be made blind."

The Pharisees believed they could see the truth, but they were blind. And the man who had been born blind was the one who could actually see truth. Not only had Jesus opened his physical eyes, but He had also opened this man's spiritual eyes. Healing is a precious gift, but the greatest and most miraculous gift is salvation.

John 9:40 and 41 continue, "Then some of the Pharisees who were with Him heard these words, and said to Him, 'Are we blind also?' Jesus said to them, 'If you were blind, you would have no sin; but now you say, "We see." Therefore your sin remains.'"

Jesus had rebuked the Pharisees. In essence, He said, "If you had been blind to the traditions preventing you from rejoicing with this man who received his sight on the Sabbath, your eyes would have been opened to see the miracle standing right in front of you!"

The greatest sight we have is not with our physical eyes but with our heart and believing on the Lord Jesus Christ and His Word. As the Holy Spirit begins to remove the blinders from our spiritual eyes, hearts, minds, and emotions, faith rises up for us to believe and receive God's Word, which is the Truth that sets us free! If Jesus has done a miracle in your life through salvation for healing, tell someone! Your testimony contains the power to defeat the devil in another person's life and open their lives to both spiritual and physical freedom!

STUDY QUESTIONS

Be diligent to present yourself approved to God, a worker
who does not need to be ashamed, rightly dividing the word of truth.
— 2 Timothy 2:15

1. Read Ephesians 1:18 in several Bible versions. In your own words, explain the benefits of spiritual eyesight in this verse.
2. Explain why the Pharisees were more concerned about *who* had healed the blind man and the fact that the healing was performed on the Sabbath than about the blind man himself and his healing.
3. What was the real reason the Pharisees were angered by the healed man's comments in John 9:30-33?

PRACTICAL APPLICATION

But be doers of the word,
and not hearers only, deceiving yourselves.
— James 1:22

Learn to listen to God's details.

1. Take a moment to reflect upon how the Lord opened your spiritual eyes. Write a brief description of that moment.
2. Think about an area where you once had spiritual blindness. Describe how your eyes were opened to Truth. What specific scripture did God use to open your eyes?

TOPIC

What's on the Other Side of Your 'Yes' to God?

SCRIPTURES

1. **John 11:1-47** — Now a certain man was sick, Lazarus of Bethany, the town of Mary and her sister Martha. It was that Mary who anointed the Lord with fragrant oil and wiped His feet with her hair, whose brother Lazarus was sick. Therefore the sisters sent to Him, saying, "Lord, behold, he whom You love is sick." When Jesus heard that, He said, "This sickness is not unto death, but for the glory of God, that the Son of God may be glorified through it." Now Jesus loved Martha and her sister and Lazarus. So, when He heard that he was sick, He stayed two more days in the place where He was. Then after this He said to the disciples, "Let us go to Judea again." The disciples said to Him, "Rabbi, lately the Jews sought to stone You, and are You going there again?" Jesus answered, "Are there not twelve hours in the day? If anyone walks in the day, he does not stumble, because he sees the light of this world. But if one walks in the night, he stumbles, because the light is not in him." These things He said, and after that He said to them, "Our friend Lazarus sleeps, but I go that I may wake him up." Then His disciples said, "Lord, if he sleeps he will get well." However, Jesus spoke of his death, but they thought that He was speaking about taking rest in sleep. Then Jesus said to them plainly, "Lazarus is dead. And I am glad for your sakes that I was not there, that you may believe. Nevertheless let us go to him." Then Thomas, who is called the Twin, said to his fellow disciples, "Let us also go, that we may die with Him."

So when Jesus came, He found that he had already been in the tomb four days. Now Bethany was near Jerusalem, about two miles away. And many of the Jews had joined the women around Martha and Mary, to comfort them concerning their brother. Then Martha, as soon as she heard that Jesus was coming, went and met Him, but Mary was sitting in the house. Now Martha said to Jesus, "Lord, if You had been here, my brother would not have died. But even now I know that whatever You ask of God, God will give You." Jesus said to her, "Your brother will rise again." Martha said to Him, "I know that he will rise again in the resurrection at the last day." Jesus said to her, "I am the resurrection and the life. He who believes in Me, though he may die, he shall live. And whoever lives and believes in Me shall never die. Do you believe this?" She said to Him, "Yes, Lord, I believe that You are the Christ, the Son of God, who is to come into the world."

And when she had said these things, she went her way and secretly called Mary her sister, saying, "The Teacher has come and is calling for you." As soon as she heard that, she arose quickly and came to Him. Now Jesus had not yet come into the town, but was in the place where Martha met Him. Then the Jews who were with her in the house, and comforting her, when they saw that Mary rose up quickly and went out, followed her, saying, "She is going to the tomb to weep there." Then, when Mary came where Jesus was, and saw Him, she fell down at His feet, saying to Him, "Lord, if You had been here, my brother would not have died." Therefore, when Jesus saw her weeping, and the Jews who came with her weeping, He groaned in the spirit and was troubled. And He said, "Where have you laid him?" They said to Him, "Lord, come and see." Jesus wept. Then the Jews said, "See how He loved him!" And some of them said, "Could not this Man, who opened the eyes of the blind, also have kept this man from dying?"

Then Jesus, again groaning in Himself, came to the tomb. It was a cave, and a stone lay against it. Jesus said, "Take away the stone." Martha, the sister of him who was dead, said to Him, "Lord, by this time there is a stench, for he has been dead four days." Jesus said to her, "Did I not say to you that if you would believe you would see the glory of God?" Then they took away the stone from the place where the dead man was lying. And Jesus lifted up His eyes and said, "Father, I thank You that You have heard Me. And I know that You always hear Me, but because of the people who are standing by I said this, that they may believe that You sent Me." Now when He had said these things, He cried with a loud voice, "Lazarus, come forth!" And he who had died came out bound hand and foot with graveclothes, and his face was wrapped with a cloth. Jesus said to them, "Loose him, and let him go." Then many of the Jews who had come to Mary, and had seen the things Jesus did, believed in Him. But some of them went away to the Pharisees and told them the things Jesus did. Then the chief priests and the Pharisees gathered a council and said, "What shall we do? For this Man works many signs."

2. **John 10:10** — The thief does not come except to steal, and to kill, and to destroy. I have come that they may have life, and that they may have it more abundantly.

SYNOPSIS

Martha and Mary sent a message to Jesus asking Him to come because their brother, Lazarus, was very ill. When Jesus received news of Lazarus' condition, He declared "This sickness will not result in death," but Lazarus died. When Jesus finally arrived at the home of Martha and Mary, they blamed Him for Lazarus' death. Even in the midst of the blame, His own emotions, and the fact that Lazarus' body had been in the tomb for four days, Jesus did not focus on the circumstances. Instead, He kept His eyes on what the Father had spoken to Him, and He raised Lazarus from the dead! Many believed in Him after He performed this miracle!

The emphasis of this lesson:

We must not be moved by the opinions of others, the impossibility of the circumstances, or our own emotions in overcoming the attacks of the enemy in our lives. Instead, we must keep our eyes on what God has spoken to our hearts and declared in His Word! On the other side of our "yes" to God's promises, a miracle is waiting!

Lazarus, the Friend of Jesus

John was originally a fisherman and was one of the first disciples Jesus called to follow Him. John was also one of the three disciples closest to Jesus. But there is another man mentioned in the Bible with whom Jesus shared a close friendship. His name was Lazarus (not to be confused with the rich man by the same name found in Luke 16, who went to hell upon his death). Lazarus, the brother of Martha and Mary, was Jesus' friend and very close to His heart.

John 11:1-3 introduces us to Lazarus: "Now a certain man was sick, Lazarus of Bethany, the town of Mary and her sister Martha. It was that Mary who anointed the Lord with fragrant oil and wiped His feet with her hair, whose brother Lazarus was sick. Therefore the sisters sent to Him, saying, 'Lord, behold, he whom You love is sick.'"

Sickness Unto Death

Mary and Martha sent word to Jesus, and said, "…He whom You love is sick" (v. 3). The Greek word for "sick" here describes a sickness that results in death. Jesus understood the seriousness of the sickness that plagued Lazarus, but He had more in store for this devoted family.

John 11:4 and 5 continues, "When Jesus heard that, He said, 'This sickness is not unto death, but for the glory of God that the Son of God may be glorified through it.' Now Jesus loved Martha and her sister and Lazarus." This verse clearly states Jesus' love for Martha, Mary, and Lazarus. You could easily insert your own name into this verse, and I could do the same! Jesus loves you, and Jesus loves me!

Let's continue with Lazarus' miraculous story: "So, when He heard that he was sick, He stayed two more days in the place where He was. Then after this He said to the disciples, 'Let us go to Judea again.' The disciples said to Him, 'Rabbi, lately the Jews sought to stone You, and are You going there again?' Jesus answered, 'Are there not twelve hours in the day? If anyone walks in the day, he does not stumble, because he sees the light of this world. But if one walks in the night, he stumbles, because the light is not in him.'"

Jesus was determined to travel to the region of Judea because Mary and Martha had sent a message to Him that their brother was very ill, but His disciples attempted to dissuade Him. They reminded Jesus that certain Jews in that area were seeking to stone Him. The disciples only focused on the negative circumstances while Jesus kept His eyes on the will of His Heavenly Father. He was confident that no harm could come to them if they traveled to Judea because they would be walking in the light of the Father's will (John 11:6-10).

Our Friend Lazarus Sleeps

Jesus knew it was time to do what His Father had asked Him to do. He said, "…'Our friend Lazarus sleeps, but I go that I may wake him up'" (John 11:11). Not understanding what Jesus was really saying, the disciples responded, "…'Lord, if he sleeps he will get well'" (v. 12).

The disciples were confused about what Jesus had just told them. They voiced, "Well, it's good that Lazarus is sleeping. Resting will help him get better soon." So Jesus had to be more direct. "…'Lazarus is dead. And I am glad for your sakes that I was not there, that you may believe. Nevertheless let us go to him'" (John 11:14,15).

The disciples thought Lazarus would wake up and everything would be fine, but Jesus had to bluntly tell them that Lazarus was dead. So now Jesus and His disciples were headed into hostile territory for a friend who had just died. It was Thomas who spoke up and revealed what was in his heart. Thomas said to his fellow disciples, "...Let us also go, that we may die with Him" (v. 16).

Thomas was willing to travel with Jesus to Judea, knowing there was a possibility that they could all be stoned by those who wanted Jesus dead. Thomas was willing to die with Jesus, but the Lord, full of life, wanted to manifest that life in the body of Lazarus.

Friend, have you ever experienced a problem and didn't know how you were going to get out of that problem? And then you asked the Lord for help, but you were unsure how He was going to answer it. But His power came — His power and His presence came and changed the whole thing. That's because He had the answer. He knew the way because He IS the way.

If we don't keep our eyes on the Lord, our thoughts and emotions can take us in the direction of disappointment, despair, and death. But Jesus never stops drawing us toward life. Jesus would not have traveled to Judea to be stoned by His enemies; His mission was to raise Lazarus from the dead and bring glory to God. Thomas was expecting the worst; he was expecting death, but Jesus was planning for a resurrection.

If You Had Only Been Here

By the time Jesus and the disciples arrived in Judea, Lazarus had been in the tomb for four days. John 11:18-27 says, "Now Bethany was near Jerusalem, about two miles away. And many of the Jews had joined the women around Martha and Mary, to comfort them concerning their brother. Then Martha, as soon as she heard that Jesus was coming, went and met Him, but Mary was sitting in the house. Now Martha said to Jesus, 'Lord, if You had been here, my brother would not have died. But even now I know that whatever You ask of God, God will give You.'"

"Jesus said to her, 'Your brother will rise again.' Martha said to Him, 'I know that he will rise again in the resurrection at the last day.' Jesus said to her, 'I am the resurrection and the life. He who believes in Me, though he may die, he shall live. And whoever lives and believes in Me shall never die. Do you believe this?' She said to Him, 'Yes, Lord, I believe that You are the Christ, the Son of God, who is to come into the world.'"

Jesus destroyed the power of death and the power of the grave through His death, burial, and resurrection. If we believe in Jesus Christ as Lord and Savior, when we die, our spirit will leave our body, but we will never die. Jesus proclaimed in verses 25 and 26, "I am the resurrection and the life. He who believes in Me, though he may die, he shall live. And whoever lives and believes in Me shall never die." What an amazing truth Jesus shared with Martha!

Even though Lazarus had been dead for four days, Jesus said he would rise again. Martha may not have understood everything Jesus had said, but she was full of faith and trusted Jesus. She responded, "Yes, Lord, I believe that You are the Christ, the Son of God, who is come into the world" (v. 27). Martha's *yes* to Jesus would result in a miracle on the other side of that *yes*!

Our miracle story continues, "And when she had said these things, she went her way and secretly called Mary her sister, saying, 'The Teacher has come and is calling for you.' As soon as she heard that, she arose quickly and came to Him. Now Jesus had not yet come into the town, but was in the place where Martha met Him. Then the Jews who were with her in the house, and comforting her, when they saw that Mary rose up quickly and went out, followed her, saying, 'She is going to the tomb to weep there.'"

"Then, when Mary came where Jesus was, and saw Him, she fell down at His feet, saying to Him, 'Lord, if You have been here, my brother would not have died.' Therefore, when Jesus saw her weeping, and the Jews who came with her weeping, He groaned in the spirit and was troubled. And He said, 'Where have you laid him?' They said to Him, 'Lord, come and see.'"

"Jesus wept. Then the Jews said, 'See how He loved him!' And some of them said, 'Could not this Man, who opened the eyes of the blind, also have kept his man from dying?'" (John 11:28-37)

First, Martha and Mary blamed Jesus for Lazarus' death, and then other people in the crowd also accused Him of not being able to prevent Lazarus' death. They all had their eyes fixed on what was happening around them — what they could see with their eyes. But Jesus had His focus on a higher, Heavenly realm.

This Sickness Will Not End in Death

When Jesus first received the message sent by Martha and Mary, He declared, "This sickness will not result in death but will bring glory to God and the Son of God will receive glory from it" (*see* John 11:4). Later, Jesus would also say, "I am glad for your sakes that I wasn't there [when Lazarus died] so you may believe and trust in Me" (*see* John 11:15).

And Jesus wants *us* to believe and not doubt His promises to us in His Word; He took our sicknesses and diseases upon His own body and the chastisement for our peace was upon Him. Anything that would try to steal our peace, Jesus took it on His own body, punished it in hell, and rose up victorious over it! We do not have to be depressed, oppressed, angry, or bitter over what someone else has done to us. We need to keep our focus on the Lord and hold on to the peace that Jesus died to provide for us!

Jesus knew He would raise His dear friend Lazarus from the dead because His eyes were on things above. He also knew that raising Lazarus from the dead would cause the Pharisees to become even more angered toward Him and they would try their best to kill Him. But Jesus had submitted Himself to the will of His Father, and He would do what His Father had called Him to do.

Not Moved

Jesus ignored the fact that Lazarus had been dead for four days. He also ignored the accusations from Martha, Mary, and the others who said it was His fault that Lazarus was dead. His response to their fear, doubt, and unbelief was a faith-filled question: "Where have you laid him?" (v. 34)

John 11:38-42 says, "Then Jesus, again groaning in Himself, came to the tomb. It was a cave, and a stone lay against it. Jesus said, 'Take away the stone.' Martha, the sister of him who was dead, said to Him, 'Lord, by this time there is a stench, for he has been dead four days.' Jesus said to her, 'Did I not say to you that if you would believe you would see the glory of God?'"

"Then they took away the stone from the place where the dead man was lying. And Jesus lifted up His eyes and said, 'Father, I thank You that You have heard Me. And I know that You always hear Me, but because of the people who are standing by I said this, that they may believe that You sent Me.'"

In addition to Lazarus, the Bible records two other instances in which people were raised from the dead by Jesus during His time on earth. In Mark 5, the 12-year-old daughter of Jairus, the ruler of the synagogue, was raised from death to life as Jesus took her by the hand.

In another instance, Jesus, His disciples, and a large crowd following them entered a city called Nain. As they approached the gate of the city, there was a dead man being carried out in an open coffin. As Jesus encountered the deceased young man's mother (who was also a widow), compassion rose up in His heart. Jesus touched the open coffin and commanded, "Young man, I say to you, arise" (Luke 7:14). Suddenly, the widow's son sat up and began to speak, being brought from death to life!

What made the circumstances of Lazarus' death different was the fact that he was Jesus' friend. When we are praying for loved ones, our emotions can have a strong influence on us. I believe one of the reasons Jesus was groaning within Himself (*see* John 11:33,38) was that He may have been pushing through both the circumstances of Lazarus' death and the accusations against Him. The Bible says that Jesus was tempted in the very same way that you and I are tempted (Hebrews 4:15). Jesus pushed through the circumstances surrounding Lazarus' death so He could identify with us when we are faced with similar circumstances.

Many Believed

The story of Lazarus' miracle continues: "Now when He [Jesus] had said these things, He cried with a loud voice, 'Lazarus, come forth!' And he who had died came out bound hand and foot with graveclothes, and his face was wrapped with a cloth. Jesus said to them, 'Loose him, and let him go.' Then many of the Jews who had come to Mary, and had seen the things Jesus did, believed in Him. But some of them went away to the Pharisees and told them the things Jesus did. Then the chief priests and the Pharisees gathered a council and said, 'What shall we do? For this Man works many signs'" (John 11:43-47).

Because of the signs that followed Jesus, many Jews believed in Him. Others went to the religious leaders to tell them about the miracles that Jesus was performing, including raising Lazarus from the dead! As a result, the religious leaders were concerned about the people's response to Jesus, and they gathered together to discuss what to do about Him.

Caiaphas, who was the Jewish high priest at the time, actually prophesied that Jesus would die and unite all of God's children scattered around the world. But from the time of Lazarus being raised from the dead, the religious leaders began to plot the death of Jesus.

Nothing stopped Jesus because He knew the will of the Father. He pushed through the unbelief and the accusations against Him, and He demonstrated that nothing is impossible to those who believe (*see* Mark 9:23). The enemy has a plan, and the fallen world has a plan — to steal, kill, and destroy. But God's plan is greater. Jesus came to give us life and give it to us more abundantly than we could ever possibly hope, dream, or imagine (*see* John 10:10). He will do the impossible — we only need to believe!

STUDY QUESTIONS

Be diligent to present yourself approved to God, a worker
who does not need to be ashamed, rightly dividing the word of truth.
— 2 Timothy 2:15

1. In John 11:4 and 5, Jesus stated, "This sickness is not unto death...." Explain why both Martha, Mary, and others blamed Jesus for the death of Lazarus.
2. In John 11:16, why did Thomas think he and the others may die with Jesus? What does this reveal about Thomas' faith and Jesus' miracle-working power?

PRACTICAL APPLICATION

But be doers of the word,
and not hearers only, deceiving yourselves.
— James 1:22

Learn to run your race with forgiveness and wisdom!

1. Recall a time when you blamed the Lord for a negative circumstance in your life. What transpired to open your eyes and correct your thinking?
2. Are there current circumstances in your life pressuring you to be in unbelief? Spend some time in the Word and find two verses that will bolster your faith against unbelief.

TOPIC

The Unseen Is Waiting To Be Seen

SCRIPTURES

1. **2 Corinthians 4:18** — While we do not look at the things which are seen, but at the things which are not seen. For the things which are seen are temporary, but the things which are not seen are eternal.

2. **Mark 6:34-39** — And Jesus, when He came out, saw a great multitude and was moved with compassion for them, because they were like sheep not having a shepherd. So He began to teach them many things. When the day was now far spent, His disciples came to Him and said, "This is a deserted place, and already the hour is late. Send them away, that they may go into the surrounding country and villages and buy themselves bread; for they have nothing to eat." But He answered and said to them, "You give them something to eat." And they said to Him, "Shall we go and buy two hundred denarii worth of bread and give them something to eat?" But He said to them, "How many loaves do you have? Go and see." And when they found out they said, "Five, and two fish." Then He commanded them to make them all sit down in groups on the green grass.

3. **Mark 6:41** — And when He had taken the five loaves and the two fish, He looked up to heaven, blessed and broke the loaves, and gave them to His disciples to set before them; and the two fish He divided among them all.

SYNOPSIS

Jesus was moved with compassion as He observed the multitude that had followed Him into the wilderness to hear Him teach. They had been listening all day, and the disciples were concerned because the people had not eaten. At Jesus' command, the disciples gathered the food they could from the crowd, but they only found five crackers and two minnows — not near enough to feed the massive crowd.

But Jesus' eyes were not fixed on what could be seen. His eyes were fixed on what could *not* be seen. He held up those five crackers and two minnows to God, and God's miracle-working power entered. All the people ate until they were filled and satisfied and there was even food left over! When we keep our eyes on the unseen of God's promises, He always does far above what we could ever imagine! The unseen is truly waiting to be seen!

The emphasis of this lesson:

Like feeding a great multitude of people as Jesus did with five little loaves and two fish, we must learn to see as God sees; we must learn to look beyond what is seen into the unseen. When we keep our focus on God and His promises, it opens the door to His miracle power in our lives and the lives of those around us!

Looking Beyond the Seen

Every born-again believer has a recreated spirit on the inside. The Holy Spirit lives within us and enables our spiritual eyes to look beyond what is seen in the natural realm. With our spiritual eyes, we are able to sense what is in the unseen realm; we can look beyond our natural senses at things that are not seen. The Bible confirms this in Second Corinthians 4:18, which says:

> **While we do not look at the things which are seen, but at the things which are not seen. For the things which are seen are temporary, but the things which are not seen are eternal.**

The gospels record many instances when Jesus was confronted with impossible situations. Although He could see what existed in the natural, He set His spiritual eyes on things not seen — where the impossible is possible!

Did Jesus realize that blind Bartimaeus was born blind and had lived his entire life in darkness (*see* Mark 10:46-52)? Of course, He did! But Jesus was not moved by the condition of Bartimaeus' eyes. Jesus had His eyes fixed on the power of God that would touch Bartimaeus' eyes and bring sight to him for the first time in his life. Beyond that, Jesus gave him new life. Bartimaeus no longer needed assistance to get from one place to another, and he no longer needed to beg for food or the basic necessities of life. God's power had given him both sight and life!

With the death of Lazarus, Jesus was not only confronted with an impossibility, but He was also blamed for that death by those closest to Him — Martha and Mary. But Jesus could see past the four days that Lazarus lay in that tomb and the decomposition of his body. He could see past the emotion of being accused of Lazarus' death. He could see past the unbelief He was hearing with His ears and seeing with His eyes. He could see past these circumstances in the natural because Jesus walked by faith and not by sight — He was looking at the things not seen (2 Corinthians 5:7).

Moved With Compassion

We can find another impossible situation recounted in Mark 6 — the story of the feeding of 5,000 people who had gathered to hear Jesus. "And Jesus, when He came out, saw a great multitude and was moved with compassion for them, because they were like sheep not having a shepherd. So He began to teach them many things. When the day was now far spent, His disciples came to Him and said, 'This is a deserted place, and already the hour is late. Send them away, that they may go into the surrounding country and villages and buy themselves bread; for they have nothing to eat.'"

"But He answered and said to them, 'You give them something to eat.' And they said to Him, 'Shall we go and buy two hundred denarii worth of bread and give them something to eat?' But He said to them, 'How many loaves do you have? Go and see.' And when they found out they said, 'Five, and two fish.' Then He commanded them to make the people all sit down in groups on the green grass" (Mark 6:34-39).

Jesus and His disciples could clearly see with their eyes and hear with their ears the vast multitude of people that had gathered to listen to Jesus. Although Mark 6:44 mentions "5,000 men," some scholars speculate that wives and children were also in attendance, so there were perhaps up to 30,000 people gathered that day.

It was the disciples who pointed out to Jesus that the people hadn't eaten all day and suggested that Jesus let the people go to nearby villages to buy some bread to eat. The disciples were not expecting the response they received from Jesus. Jesus said, "*You* feed them" (*see* v. 37).

They answered Jesus, "Do you want us to go buy bread? We don't have nearly enough money!" But, again, Jesus' eyes were not fixed on the number of people or lack of resources. Jesus sent them out among the people to collect whatever food they could find, and they returned with five loaves and two fish.

Five Crackers and Two Minnows

Mark 6:41 continues, "And when He had taken the five loaves and two fish, He looked up to heaven, blessed and broke the loaves, and gave them to His disciples...."

Those two "loaves" were actually two *crackers*, and the two "fish" were actually two *minnows*. In other words, it's something one may have found in a child's lunch sack. Can you imagine trying to feed so many people with so little? But Jesus was not looking at what He could see with His eyes, He was looking at things not visible to His natural eyes.

Nothing Is Impossible

The things we can see with our natural eyes are temporal, but the things we cannot see are eternal. If we live our lives according to what we can see with our physical eyes and hear with our physical ears, we will not experience much of God's miraculous power that He's made available to us.

Consider Moses. He could have focused on the circumstances surrounding him. He knew God had called him to deliver the children of Israel from bondage in Egypt. They had been slaves for 400 years, yet God had instructed Moses to deliver God's people from the bondage of the Egyptians. It looked impossible in the natural, but Moses looked to God, whom he could not see with his eyes. As a result, God performed many miracles through Moses on behalf of the children of Israel! After ten plagues, Pharoah finally let God's people go free!

In Lesson 1, I mentioned my friend who had a cancerous tumor in her womb. The doctors could only see that tumor and that it needed to be removed. But my friend was looking at the unseen, and the God of the unseen realm caused His miraculous power to manifest, and that tumor completely disappeared!

I also knew a woman who had no idea how she was going to be able to pay for her daughter's college education. But she continued to pursue that direction because she knew it was God's will for her daughter.

Every morning this woman would take her dog for a walk, and she would go in a certain direction. Then one morning she decided to walk in a different direction. She met a woman whom she had never met, and they began to visit. Their conversation led to a discussion about colleges, and this complete stranger shared with her a way for her daughter's tuition to be completely paid for! This mother did not have her eyes focused on the lack of funds for her daughter to go to college — she was focused on God, her Provider. And God's miraculous power came on the scene resulting in provision for her daughter's college tuition!

I have another friend who had a 12-year-old daughter who contracted a horrific disease. She took her to the hospital and learned that many other children had been infected with the same sickness. One by one, the other children were dying. Fear tried to grip my friend's heart, but she chose to look at what is not seen — God's miracle-working power! She began speaking to that fear and declaring, "Fear, you will not have me! I am looking to God's promises and keeping my eyes fixed on life and not death!" She and her family prayed for her daughter and the very next day, the condition left the young girl's body, and she was released from the hospital — completely well!

Seeing as God Sees

You may be facing a situation that looks impossible. Maybe the bank is saying there is no way out of your financial circumstances except to declare bankruptcy, or maybe doctors have said death is the only conclusion to the symptoms in your body. Whatever your impossible situation is, if you will turn your focus to Him and place your faith in Him and His Word, His unseen power will be brought into your impossible situation and bring freedom and deliverance!

David was just a shepherd boy. His father sent him to check on his older brothers and take them provisions. David's brothers were fighting with the Israelite army against the Philistines and a formidable enemy warrior named Goliath (*see* 1 Samuel 17). When David arrived at the front lines and asked what would be given to the man who defeated Goliath, his oldest brother, Eliab, mocked him and said, "Why are you here? Go back to those sheep you watch over."

Sometimes older siblings can get an attitude about their younger siblings. It isn't right but it does happen. Eliab looked at David as an unsuccessful and arrogant younger brother — a mere shepherd boy. But David was looking to the unseen God, and God saw much more than a shepherd boy; He saw a giant-killer! And God also saw a humble, powerful king and a man after His own heart.

And then there's Daniel. Daniel was a young man who lost his family, his culture, his name, and his language when he was taken captive and moved to a foreign land. Daniel was enslaved and his circumstances probably looked impossible to him. But Daniel did not keep his focus on what could be seen and felt with his five senses. He kept his eyes on the unseen God whom he served. God did not see a weak captive who was too young to be of any influence; God saw a leader and a beloved advisor to four powerful kings of the Babylonian kingdom. (*Read* Daniel's complete story in the Old Testament book of Daniel.)

Esther was a young Jewish girl who had been orphaned. Like Daniel, she lost her family, her culture, and her language — she had lost everything! But she was crowned queen and then learned of a plot to eliminate all Jews from the land. Although she knew going before the king without being invited could result in her death, she turned her eyes toward the unseen God. His power came into a very dark situation for the children of Israel and God used Esther to deliver this nation. (*Read* Esther's complete story in the Old Testament book of Esther.)

When the apostle Paul was in a Roman prison, he did not look at what he could see surrounding him. His eyes were on the God of the unseen realm. Scholars recorded that the jail where Paul was imprisoned was actually part of the city's sewage system. Paul stood in raw sewage as he was bound in chains. He was surrounded by death. As Paul continued to focus on the unseen, he wrote the book of Philippians and used the words "joy" or "joyful" 19 times! God turned Paul into a joy-giver! Even while in the worst of conditions, Paul wrote, "Rejoice in the Lord always. Again I say, rejoice" (Philippians 4:4)!

And Jesus did not focus on His wounds while on the cross. His body was so torn and marred that He had become unrecognizable. His body was ripped, bruised, and so lacerated that His muscles were exposed. If we had been there, we would have witnessed Jesus trying to push up on the nails in His feet to catch a breath. What did God see in this moment? He saw the resurrected Christ and a Church filled with people whose sins had been completely blotted out and the power of death destroyed. What appeared to be the end of the Church was the total destruction of death, hell, and the grave!

Jesus was looking at the joy set before Him — you and me! The Bible says that a day is approaching when every knee will bow, and every tongue will confess that Jesus is Lord

We must not look at ourselves through natural eyes. We need to see ourselves as God sees us — with the power and potential of God on the inside who is capable of the impossible. We must see ourselves with the boldness to lead people to the Lord, the potential to help people in their difficult situations, and the ability to change lives by the power of God inside us!

If we keep our eyes fixed on our Savior and spend time in His Word, we will believe what He says about us as His children.

- We will believe it was by His stripes that we *are* healed (*see* Isaiah 53:5)!

- We will believe we are more than conquerors through Christ Jesus (*see* Romans 8:37)!

- We will believe that God is for us, and no one can be against us (*see* Romans 8:31)!

- We will believe that no weapon formed against us will prosper and every tongue that rises up against us will be silenced (*see* Isaiah 54:17)!

- We will believe all things are possible to us who believe (*see* Mark 9:23)!

A prayer for you: *I pray for you right now, in the precious name of Jesus, that you will not just look with your natural eyes, but you will look from your heart and to the unseen and say, "God, I recognize that You are powerful in my life. I give you my life once again. Help me to recognize and agree with what You have put on the inside of me. In Jesus' name. Amen."*

STUDY QUESTIONS

Be diligent to present yourself approved to God, a worker who does not need to be ashamed, rightly dividing the word of truth.
— 2 Timothy 2:15

1. Describe one instance in which Jesus faced an impossible situation and how He reacted to it. How can you apply His example to your own personal life today?
2. Why do you think Jesus told the disciples to feed the multitude and what did His example teach them?

PRACTICAL APPLICATION

But be doers of the word,
and not hearers only, deceiving yourselves.
— James 1:22

Don't let the enemy push you out of your race!

1. List one character in the Bible who did not focus on what was seen and explain how their example has inspired your life personally.
2. In what area of your life are you currently looking through your natural eyes rather than your spiritual eyes? Find at least one verse that brings truth to open your spiritual eyes.

Notes

Notes

CLAIM YOUR FREE RESOURCE!

As a way of introducing you further to the teaching ministry of Rick Renner, we would like to send you FREE of charge his teaching, "How To Receive a Miraculous Touch From God" on CD or as an MP3 download.

How To Receive
a Miraculous Touch From God
Rick Renner

CD36

RENNER

In His earthly ministry, Jesus commonly healed *all* who were sick of *all* their diseases. In this profound message, learn about the manifold dimensions of Christ's wisdom, goodness, power, and love toward all humanity who came to Him in faith with their needs.

☑ YES, I want to receive Rick Renner's monthly teaching letter!

Simply scan the QR code to claim this resource or go to:
renner.org/claim-your-free-offer

Connect

WITH US!

www.ingramcontent.com/pod-product-compliance
Lightning Source LLC
Chambersburg PA
CBHW071653040426
42452CB00009B/1855